LEVEL

3

Fact Reader

Erupt!

100 FUN Facts About Volcanoes

Joan Marie Galat

NATIONAL GEOGRAPHIC

Washington, D.C.

For Dad, a geologist and a rock in my life —J.M.G.

Copyright © 2017 National Geographic Partners, LLC

Published by National Geographic Partners, LLC, Washington, D.C. 20036. All rights reserved. Reproduction in whole or in part without written permission of the publisher is prohibited.

NATIONAL GEOGRAPHIC and Yellow Border Design are trademarks of the National Geographic Society, used under license.

Designed by Amanda Larsen

Library of Congress Cataloging-in-Publication Data

Names: Galat, Joan Marie, 1963- author.
Title: Erupt! : 100 fun facts about volcanoes / Joan Marie Galat.
Description: Washington, D.C. : National Geographic Children's Books, 2017. | Series: National Geographic kids fact readers | Includes index. | Audience: Age 6 to 9. | Audience: K to grade 3.
Identifiers: LCCN 2016051354 (print) | LCCN 2017016844 (ebook) | ISBN 9781426329128 (e-book) | ISBN 9781426329111 (hardcover) | ISBN 9781426329104 (paperback)
Subjects: LCSH: Volcanoes--Juvenile literature. | BISAC: JUVENILE NONFICTION / Readers / Beginner. | JUVENILE NONFICTION / Science & Nature / Earth Sciences / Earthquakes & Volcanoes.
Classification: LCC QE521.3 (ebook) | LCC QE521.3 .G357 2017 (print) | DDC 551.21--dc23
LC record available at https://lccn.loc .gov/2016051354

Photo Credits

Cover, Stephen Belcher/Minden Pictures; 1, Arctic-Images/Getty Images; 3, DU BOISBERRANGER Jean/hemis.fr/Getty Images; 4 (UP), Dan Ballard/Getty Images; 4 (LO LE), rtem/Shutterstock; 4 (LO RT), Prof. Stewart Lowther/Science Photo Library/Getty Images; 5 (UP), Grant Dixon/Getty Images; 5 (CTR LE), Toshi Sasaki/Getty Images; 5 (CTR RT), Jiri Hera/Shutterstock; 5 (LO), Jonathan Blair/Getty Images; 6–7, Salvatore Allegra Photography/Getty Images; 9, photoDISC; 11, Stuart Armstrong; 12, Kevin Thrash/Getty Images; 13, Mary Van de Ven/Getty Images; 14 (LE), Chris Bickford/National Geographic Creative; 14 (RT), MichaelUtech/Getty Images; 15 (UP), Auscape/UIG/Getty Images; 15 (LO), Santiago Rodríguez Fontoba/Dreamstime; 16–17, Buena Vista Images/Getty Images; 18, Fotos593/Shutterstock; 19 (UP), bilwissedition Ltd. & Co. KG/Alamy Stock Photo; 19 (CTR), Herbert K. Kane; 19 (LO), Culture Club/Getty Images; 20–21, G. Brad Lewis/Getty Images; 22, Hans Strand/Getty Images; 23, Roger Bacon/Reuters/Alamy Stock Photo; 24 (LE), Toshi Sasaki/Getty Images; 24 (RT), filmlandscape/Getty Images; 25, Eachat/Getty Images; 26–27, Matthew Oldfield/Science Source; 28, Martin Bernetti/AFP/Getty Images; 29, Calvin Hall/Getty Images; 30, Athit Perawongmetha/Getty Images; 31, G. Brad Lewis/Getty Images; 33, Ron Dahlquist/Getty Images; 34 (LE), Harry Taylor/Getty Images; 34 (RT), everything possible/Shutterstock; 35, Gary Hincks/Science Source; 36, atese/Getty Images; 37 (UP), Chris Clor/Getty Images; 37 (LO), Eric Isselée/Shutterstock; 38, Detlev van Ravenswaay/Science Source; 39, NASA/JPL/University of Arizona; 40, Jacques Langevin/Sygma/Sygma via Getty Images; 41 (UP), Cosmin Manci/Shutterstock; 41 (LO), Leigh Marsh; 42–43, Blueplace/Getty Images; 44 (UP), vvoe/Shutterstock; 44 (CTR), Evans/Getty Images; 44 (LO), Somchai Som/Shutterstock; 45 (UP), MarcAndreLeTourneux/Shutterstock; 45 (CTR), Hilary Andrews/NG Staff; 45 (LO), NASA images/Shutterstock; various (top border of page), T.Thinnapat/Shutterstock

National Geographic supports K–12 educators with ELA Common Core Resources. Visit natgeoed.org/commoncore for more information.

Printed in the United States of America
17/WOR/1

Table of Contents

1 Heavy ashfall can make it impossible to breathe.

2 The powdery ash that volcanoes eject can float around the world.

3 Mount St. Helens, in Washington State, U.S.A., caused the largest landslide known on Earth when it erupted.

4 Magma flows to Earth's surface because it is lighter than the solid rock around it.

5 Lava can reach 2,000 degrees Fahrenheit—four times hotter than your kitchen oven!

6 An umbrella won't help! Lava blown from a volcano hardens into solid rock in the air, and the pieces fall like rain.

7 In the United States alone, 80 volcanoes have erupted once or more in the past 500 years.

8 The heat from lava causes the plants it buries to release gases and explode.

9 Volcanoes can change the weather.

25 HOT FACTS ABOUT VOLCANOES

10

Mount St. Helens destroyed eight bridges when it erupted.

11

When lava reaches the ocean, it cools rapidly. It breaks down to form black sand beaches.

12

A volcanic eruption can blow apart a mountain.

13

Lava that cools into rough pieces is called aa (AH-ah).

14

Ash in the sky can make day as dark as night.

15

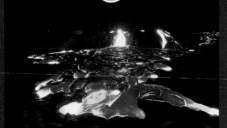

Most lava moves slow enough for people to escape it.

16

When it explodes from a volcano, runny lava may form cow-pie "bombs" that splat into rough pancake shapes.

17

When the Icelandic volcano Eyjafjallajökull erupted in 2010, ash forced airports as far away as mainland Europe to shut down for almost a week.

18

Water warmed by volcanoes is used to heat homes in Iceland.

19

Rich volcanic soil is excellent for growing crops.

20

Volcanoes eject bombs— semi-molten pieces of lava— and solid lava chunks called blocks.

21

A pyroclastic flow is a fast-moving mix of hot gas, ash, and rock that can destroy everything in its path.

22

A volcano can flatten a forest.

23

Lava that hardens into a smooth, ropy surface is called pahoehoe (paw-HOE-EE-hoe-ee).

24

25

Volcanic bombs and blocks can be as small as your fist or as big as a house.

Earth's largest land volcano, Mauna Loa in Hawaii, U.S.A., is more than 10 miles high from its base on the seafloor to its top.

CHAPTER 1

OUR FIERY WORLD

Besides Stromboli, a volcano erupts somewhere on Earth EVERY WEEK.

SEVERAL TIMES AN HOUR, LAVA SHOOTS OUT of a volcano in Italy called Stromboli.

Stromboli has been spewing gas and spitting molten rock for more than 2,000 years! It is one of Earth's most active volcanoes. Full eruptions can occur from only minutes to hours apart.

Volcanoes begin deep underground. Hot liquid rock pushes upward. It escapes in a powerful burst. Lava, ash, and steam pour from the mountain. In an instant, the landscape around the volcano changes.

A volcano can destroy an ENTIRE TOWN.

Earth's surface is made of giant slabs of constantly moving rock.

These giant pieces of rock, or tectonic plates, cover the globe. They form the crust, our planet's thin outer layer.

The crust floats on the mantle—an 1,800-mile-thick layer of hot liquid, or molten, rock called magma. The mantle flows just enough to slowly move the plates.

The MAGMA THAT FORMS MOST VOLCANOES comes from just a few miles below Earth's surface.

Gravity causes the heavy plates to sink slowly into the mantle. Inch by inch, the plates have crept along for hundreds of millions of years.

TECTONIC PLATES are hundreds to thousands of miles across and 10 to 125 miles thick.

The Alps were formed by tectonic plates crashing together.

Beneath Your Feet

Moving tectonic plates can make MOUNTAINS AND VOLCANOES.

Tectonic plates don't just float along. They bump, pull apart, and slide below one another. Plates crashing together can buckle the ground to form mountains.

A volcano can form when a tectonic plate is forced downward into the mantle.

First, heat and pressure inside Earth melt part of the plate, forming magma. The new magma creates pressure. The pressure helps force the magma upward.

Tectonic Plates in the Ocean

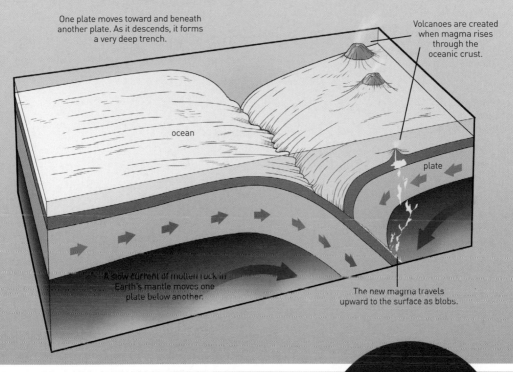

One plate moves toward and beneath another plate. As it descends, it forms a very deep trench.

Volcanoes are created when magma rises through the oceanic crust.

ocean

plate

A slow current of molten rock in Earth's mantle moves one plate below another.

The new magma travels upward to the surface as blobs.

Heat inside Earth can create HOT SPRINGS AND BUBBLING MUD POOLS around the volcano.

If a spot in Earth's crust has a hole, called a vent, molten rock and ash can escape. That's a volcano!

When the rising magma escapes through the top of the volcano's vent, it gets a new name. Now it is lava.

A collapsing volcano can form a caldera MORE THAN 60 MILES WIDE.

WHEN HOT MAGMA RISES THROUGH THE CRUST, instead of at the edges of tectonic plates, it is called a hot spot.

Volcanic mountains can form when heat and pressure, miles below Earth's crust, form magma that rises through cracks in the crust. Shallow areas of magma collect beneath the crust and ooze upward through the cracks.

If the magma reaches a vent, a hole that runs from deep underground to Earth's surface, a volcanic eruption occurs. Some eruptions make an explosion. Others cause lava to simply flow out. A violent explosion can cause a volcano to collapse and form a giant bowl-shaped area called a caldera.

Some explosive eruptions form craters. They are rounder and smaller than calderas.

Cones and Domes

There are four main types of volcanoes.

Cinder cone volcanoes form when exploding lava hardens into glassy rock fragments. The falling cinders create a steep, cone-shaped hill around the vent.

cinder cone volcano

volcano with lava dome

Cinders contain gases that look like BUBBLES FROZEN IN ROCK.

composite volcano

Composite volcanoes

form mountains with separate layers of lava, ash, cinders, blocks, and bombs.

shield volcano

Shield volcanoes form

when lava flows in all directions. The liquid rock hardens into a large wide cone instead of a cone with steep sides.

Volcanoes with lava domes

form when lava is too thick and sticky to flow very far. Towering domes may reach more than half a mile high.

Some lava domes have been GROWING FOR 100 YEARS.

15

CHAPTER 2

DANGER!

Mount Vesuvius erupted nearly 2,000 YEARS AGO.

Italy shook when Mount Vesuvius exploded in A.D. 79. Romans ran from the mountain as lava flowed over two entire towns—Pompeii (pom-PAY) and

Pompeii today

16

Herculaneum (HERK-yoo-LANE-ee-um). The volcano quickly buried Pompeii in several feet of ash and small pieces of rock. The ash preserved buildings and objects just as they were when it happened. Fiery flows struck Herculaneum. The explosion was so fast, people didn't have time to escape. Thousands of people lost their lives. As the ash hardened, it froze people's everyday lives into rocky scenes.

The word "volcano" comes from THE ANCIENT ROMAN GOD OF FIRE—Vulcan.

People have known volcanoes are dangerous for a long time. But they haven't always known what causes them to erupt. Ancient cultures made up different stories to explain why mountains spit fire and hurl rocks. Some blamed volcanoes on angry gods or monsters.

Hephaestus, the GREEK GOD OF FIRE, was a blacksmith. Early Greeks believed you could tell he was working when fire came out of the mountain.

In one myth, a hundred-headed beast called Typhon lived below Mount Etna in Sicily. People thought the volcano erupted when Typhon got angry. They said lava and hot rocks poured from his hundred mouths.

In Hawaii, Polynesians told of a goddess named Pele (PAY-lay) who lived in the volcano Kilauea (kill-ah-WAY-ya). Pele had a bad temper. When she got mad, Kilauea erupted.

Pele

THIN STRANDS OF VOLCANIC GLASS are called Pele's hair.

Typhon

Ancient cultures were right to fear lava, but not because of monsters. Lava is hot enough to destroy everything it touches. It can melt shoes and burn skin. Hot lava can start fires and cause water to boil and splatter.

Rivers of lava flowing away from a volcano's vent CAN FORM HOLLOW TUBES.

LAVA TUBES CAN FORM CAVES large enough to walk through.

LAVA CAN
REMAIN HOT
for days or
even years.

More Than Lava

Boom! When a volcano erupts, thick gray ash fills the sky. Volcanic ash forms when gases trapped in magma blast outward. The cooling rock shatters into dust. Ash and hot gases can whoosh together down a

Volcanic ash
DOES NOT DISSOLVE IN WATER.

mountain in a dangerous flow, traveling up to 125 miles an hour. The flow, called a pyroclastic flow,

A street in Plymouth, Montserrat (West Indies), is covered in ash after volcanic eruptions.

knocks down or buries everything it touches. It can even travel uphill.

Ash is made up of minerals, rocks, and sharp volcanic glass. It can be fine or coarse. Fine ash is powdery. Coarse ash is like sand.

Clouds of ash can interfere with the MIGRATION OF BIRDS.

Ash may not seem as dangerous as lava, but wind can blow it thousands of miles away from a volcano. It can cause airplanes and other machinery to crash or break.

As if lava and ash weren't enough, volcanic eruptions release gases, too!

Without much warning, gases trapped in lava can burst out. The violent explosions scatter lava into the air. If the lava is more runny, gases leave with less fuss. They simply cause the lava to ooze out and down the mountain.

HOT GASES MAY WHISTLE OR HISS as they escape vents called fumaroles.

Sometimes gas escapes from cooling rock so fast, it makes the rock full of holes. This rock is called pumice.

pumice

Lava releases toxic gases that form CLOUDS OF ACID.

MOST VOLCANIC GAS IS WATER VAPOR, but volcanoes also contain poisonous gases.

Volcanic gases may settle over low ground or travel through lava tubes. Lava that reaches the ocean can form misty clouds of hydrochloric acid and steam called laze.

If volcanic gases dissolve into liquids, THEY CAN FORM ACID LAKES.

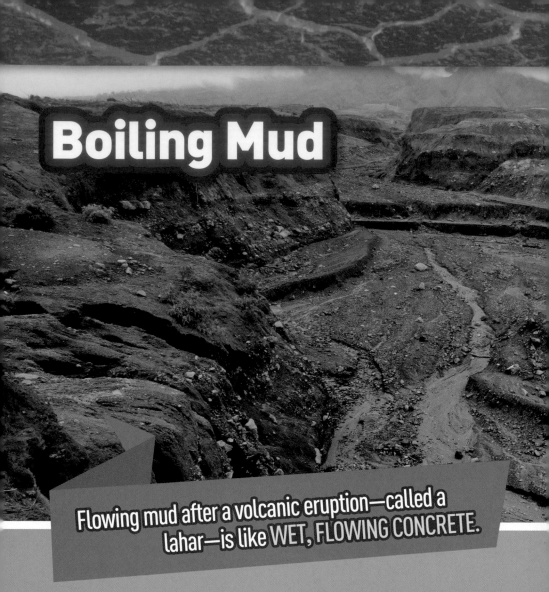

Boiling Mud

Flowing mud after a volcanic eruption—called a lahar—is like WET, FLOWING CONCRETE.

The volcano appears to grow quiet. The eruption is over. Nothing escapes its vent—no lava, no rocks, no ash. Is the danger over? No! A river of mud, ash, and rock fragments may gush down the mountain. The flow may be cold or boiling

LAHARS ARE POWERFUL! They can pick up and move rocks, soil, plants, and even buildings.

hot. It travels fast, reaching speeds of up to 40 miles an hour.

Even long after an eruption, heavy rainfall may cause ash, soil, and loose rocks to wash down a steep mountain. The lahar can destroy everything in its path.

Volcano Weather

Gases escaping from hot lava create VOLCANIC SMOG, called vog.

The change begins when large ash clouds block the sun. With less sunlight, the air becomes cooler.

Water droplets collect around ash particles. Soon raindrops begin to fall. Thunder rumbles and lightning crackles.

When a very large volcano erupts, lightning may form in the plume escaping the vent. When volcanic lightning and ash happen at the same time, it is called a dirty thunderstorm.

Orange, red, yellow! Volcanic ash in the atmosphere can lead to PRETTY SUNRISES AND SUNSETS.

CHAPTER 3

VOLCANO DETECTIVES

VOLCANOES CAN BLOW THEIR TOPS WITHOUT WARNING. But most of the time, they give clues that they may erupt.

One sign that a volcano eruption might be coming is if the ground shakes. Earthquakes can mean magma is on the rise. The flowing magma may heat the ground and push it outward. Scientists place sensors near volcanoes to measure pushed-out ground and watch for signs of shaking.

A volcanic eruption with a plume 19 miles or higher is called a COLOSSAL ERUPTION.

Volcanoes may give out signs for a long time before they actually erupt.

Scientists also measure the warmth of water and escaping gases near the volcano. Watch out! Rising temperatures in either the water or the gases can mean an eruption might soon occur.

Faking Sleep

A volcano is "active" if it is erupting, if clues signal it might blow its top again, or if it has erupted at least once in the past 10,000 years. A volcano is "extinct" if scientists believe it will not erupt again.

If scientists think a quiet volcano may erupt again, it's called a "dormant" volcano. A dormant volcano can be quiet for 10,000 years or more.

The RING OF FIRE is a region of mountain-building volcanoes in the Pacific Ocean.

It's important for scientists to keep an eye on volcanoes. They study

DIAMOND HEAD, on the Hawaiian island Oahu, is an extinct volcano with a 300,000-YEAR-OLD crater.

areas of old lava and the land around a volcano to see how the volcano has behaved in the past. These clues tell them what a volcano might do next.

Treasures Inside Earth

If scientists see a type of rock called kimberlite, they know they might find diamonds, too. Kimberlite rock begins as a rare type of magma found about 100 miles below Earth's surface.

kimberlite rock

diamond

KIMBERLITE VOLCANOES ARE RARE. None have erupted since people started keeping records.

When a diamond is cut and polished, it can be used in jewelry.

The rising magma is like an underground elevator. It picks up passengers like fragments of rock and mineral, silt, and even diamonds. These underground treasures reach Earth's surface when the magma erupts from a carrot-shaped vent called a pipe.

Volcanic pipes can be several miles deep and hundreds of yards wide. ➜

pipe

Volcanoes All Around

Far below the ocean waves, HUGE MOUNTAIN RANGES CROSS THE SEABED. Some are volcanoes!

Scientists believe that nearly 75 PERCENT OF VOLCANIC ERUPTIONS occur underwater.

You may find volcanoes anywhere on Earth's surface, but they show up in some strange places, too.

Submarine volcanoes, which are underwater, can erupt as tectonic plates slowly move apart—a process called seafloor spreading. If a submarine volcano is near the surface, steam and rock shoot up from the water.

Sharks have been found swimming AROUND SUBMARINE VOLCANOES, but not during an eruption!

If the mountain is deeper, water cools the lava before it reaches the surface. The lava turns to pillow-shaped rock. If the lava cools very fast, it will shatter into broken rock and sand.

OLYMPUS MONS is large enough to hold all the Hawaiian Islands.

OLYMPUS MONS STATS

- 374-mile-diameter base
- 16 miles high
- 50-mile-wide caldera
- Last erupted millions of years ago

Olympus Mons, on Mars, is the LARGEST KNOWN VOLCANO IN OUR SOLAR SYSTEM.

Volcanoes are found in space, too! Olympus Mons is an extinct shield volcano on Mars. It's the highest mountain on the planet, and it's a hundred times larger than Earth's biggest volcano!

About the same size as Earth's moon, Jupiter's moon Io has the most active volcanoes of any moon or planet in our solar system. Spacecraft took pictures of one of its volcanoes shooting out gas and melted rock. The plume rose about 250 miles high!

The last volcanoes to erupt on Earth's moon were active THREE BILLION YEARS AGO.

This photo of Io shows a volcanic plume (blue eruption on left).

Living Near the Danger Zone

Do you live near a mountain that might erupt? Millions do, and if you live in or visit a danger zone, you need to know what to do in an emergency.

Volcanoes can be dangerous even when they're out of sight. Violent lahars have been known to flow for MORE THAN 50 MILES.

Volcano Safety Tips

If a volcano is erupting:
- Follow authority's orders to leave the area.
- If trapped outside, move to high ground.
- Avoid areas downwind and downriver.
- Wear goggles and a dust mask when ash is falling.
- If inside, close windows and doors.
- Look for news updates to know when it is safe to go outside.

The first animals to return to Mount St. Helens were SOME SPECIES OF BEETLE AND SPIDER.

THE WORD VOLCANO IN OTHER LANGUAGES:
Hawaiian – *lua pele*
Icelandic – *eldfjall*
Spanish – *volcán*

A species of shrimp that HAS EYES ON ITS BACK has been found in magma-heated water under the ocean.

MORE THAN 600 MILLION PEOPLE
live on or near an active volcano.

People know long periods of time may pass between eruptions and that scientists can warn them if a volcano becomes dangerous. Although there is danger, people who live near volcanoes come back after an eruption.

The area's soil is rich with nutrients from lava that broke down over thousands of years. Volcanic rocks can contain metals and minerals like lead, copper, gold, and silver. Heat from volcanoes can be used to create energy for electricity. Most of all, though, people return because the volcano is home.

Mount Etna, Italy

1 Seafloor spreading creates new crust under oceans.

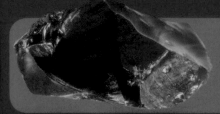

2 Volcanoes form dense, dark glass called obsidian.

3 The Big Island of Hawaii is made of active volcanoes formed over a hot spot.

4 Scientists who study volcanoes are called volcanologists.

5 Violent volcanoes can shoot ash more than 100,000 feet into the sky.

6 Volcanoes take thousands of years to form, but Parícutin, in Mexico, grew almost 165 feet in one night.

7 The rotten egg smell near some volcanoes is caused by a gas called hydrogen sulfide.

8 The eruption of Krakatoa in Indonesia in 1883 could be heard almost 3,000 miles away.

9 One eruption sent pumice flying as far as 16 miles away.

10 The moon is sometimes called "dead" because its volcanoes are extinct.

25 MORE HOT FACTS ABOUT VOLCANOES

11

Edinburgh Castle in Scotland is built on an extinct volcano.

12

Wet ash can weigh down a tree enough to make it fall.

13

Magma collects in underground chambers below volcanoes.

14

Earthquakes below volcanoes can sound like thunder.

15

Volcanologists can predict if a volcano will erupt within days or months.

16

Volcanic craters can hold lakes of lava. These rare lakes create a bright red glow at night.

17

Pumice can be light enough to float on water!

18

Most volcanoes release smelly sulfur dioxide, which has the same odor as a just-lit match.

19

Volcanoes can form geysers—holes where hot water bursts out at regular intervals.

20

Native Americans used sharp volcanic obsidian for arrowheads, cutting tools, and trading.

21

Lava domes that grow too fast can collapse.

22

A submarine volcano can cause a tsunami.

23

Millions of tourists visit volcanoes every year.

24

Venus has more than 1,600 volcanoes. Scientists don't know if any of the volcanoes are active, but they have seen the levels of sulfur dioxide increase in Venus's atmosphere.

25

Volcanoes can cause avalanches of snow, ice, trees, and volcanic matter.

VOLCANO FACTS ROUNDUP

BOOM!
You're erupting with volcano knowledge. Did you catch all 100 facts?

1. Heavy ashfall can make it impossible to breathe. 2. The powdery ash that volcanoes eject can float around the world. 3. Mount St. Helens, in Washington State, U.S.A., caused the largest landslide known on Earth when it erupted. 4. Magma flows to Earth's surface because it is lighter than the solid rock around it. 5. Lava can reach 2,000 degrees Fahrenheit—four times hotter than your kitchen oven! 6. Lava blown from a volcano hardens into solid rock in the air, and the pieces fall like rain. 7. In the United States alone, 80 volcanoes have erupted once or more in the past 500 years. 8. The heat from lava causes the plants it buries to release gases and explode. 9. Volcanoes can change the weather. 10. Mount St. Helens destroyed eight bridges when it erupted. 11. When lava reaches the ocean, it cools rapidly. It breaks down to form black sand beaches. 12. A volcanic eruption can blow apart a mountain. 13. Lava that cools into rough pieces is called aa. 14. Ash in the sky can make day as dark as night. 15. Most lava moves slow enough for people to escape it. 16. When it explodes from a volcano, runny lava may form cow-pie "bombs" that splat into rough pancake shapes. 17. When the Icelandic volcano Eyjafjallajökull erupted in 2010, ash forced airports as far away as mainland Europe to shut down for almost a week. 18. Water warmed by volcanoes is used to heat homes in Iceland. 19. Rich volcanic soil is excellent for growing crops. 20. Volcanoes eject bombs—semi-molten pieces of lava—and solid lava chunks called blocks. 21. A pyroclastic flow is a fast-moving mix of hot gas, ash, and rock that can destroy everything in its path. 22. A volcano can flatten a forest. 23. Lava that hardens into a smooth, ropy surface is called pahoehoe. 24. Earth's largest land volcano, Mauna Loa in Hawaii, U.S.A., is more than 10 miles high from its base on the seafloor to its top. 25. Volcanic bombs and blocks can be as small as your fist or as big as a house. 26. Several times an hour, lava shoots out of a volcano in Italy called Stromboli. 27. Besides Stromboli, a volcano erupts somewhere on Earth every week. 28. A volcano can destroy an entire town. 29. The magma that forms most volcanoes comes from just a few miles below Earth's surface. 30. Tectonic plates are hundreds to thousands of miles across and 10 to 125 miles thick. 31. Moving tectonic plates can make mountains and volcanoes. 32. Heat inside Earth can create hot springs and bubbling mud pools around the volcano. 33. A collapsing volcano can form a caldera more than 60 miles wide. 34. When hot magma rises through the crust, instead of at the edges of tectonic plates, it is called a hot spot. 35. Lava turns to solid rock as it cools. Each eruption spreads more lava and makes the mountain grow larger. 36. Cinders contain gases that look like bubbles frozen in rock. 37. Some lava domes have been growing for 100 years. 38. Mount Vesuvius erupted nearly 2,000 years ago. 39. The word "volcano" comes from the ancient Roman god of fire—Vulcan. 40. Hephaestus, the Greek god of fire, was a blacksmith. Early Greeks believed you could

tell he was working when fire came out of the mountain. 41. Thin strands of volcanic glass are called Pele's hair. 42. Rivers of lava flowing away from a volcano's vent can form hollow tubes. 43. Lava tubes can form caves large enough to walk through. 44. Lava can remain hot for days or even years. 45. Volcanic ash does not dissolve in water. 46. Clouds of ash can interfere with the migration of birds. 47. Hot gases may whistle or hiss as they escape vents called fumaroles. 48. Lava releases toxic gases that form clouds of acid. 49. Most volcanic gas is water vapor, but volcanoes also contain poisonous gases. 50. If volcanic gases dissolve into liquids, they can form acid lakes. 51. Flowing mud after a volcanic eruption—called a lahar—is like wet, flowing concrete. 52. Lahars are powerful! They can pick up and move rocks, soil, plants, and even buildings. 53. Gases escaping from hot lava create volcanic smog called vog. 54. An erupting volcano can change the weather. 55. Volcanic ash in the atmosphere can lead to pretty sunrises and sunsets. 56. Volcanoes can blow their tops without warning. But most of the time, they give clues that they may erupt. 57. A volcanic eruption with a plume 19 miles or higher is called a colossal eruption. 58. A volcano can be "active," "extinct," or "dormant." 59. The Ring of Fire is a region of mountain-building volcanoes in the Pacific Ocean. 60. Diamond Head, on the Hawaiian Island of Oahu, is an extinct volcano with a 300,000-year-old crater. 61. Rising magma can bring diamonds to Earth's surface. 62. Kimberlite volcanoes are rare. None have erupted since people started keeping records. 63. Far below the ocean waves, huge mountain ranges cross the seabed. Some are volcanoes! 64. Scientists believe that nearly 75 percent of volcanic eruptions occur underwater. 65. Submarine volcanoes make islands when they reach the ocean's surface. 66. Sharks have been found swimming around submarine volcanoes, but not during an eruption. 67. Olympus Mons is large enough to hold all the Hawaiian Islands. 68. Olympus Mons is the largest known volcano in our solar system. 69. Different kinds of active volcanoes can be found on some of the moons of Jupiter, Saturn, and Neptune. 70. The last volcanoes to erupt on Earth's moon were active three billion years ago. 71. Violent lahars have been known to flow for more than 50 miles. 72. The first animals to return to Mount St. Helens were some species of beetle and spider. 73. In other languages, "volcano" is *lua pele* (Hawaiian); *eldfjall* (Icelandic); *volcán* (Spanish). 74. A species of shrimp that has eyes on its back has been found in magma-heated water under the ocean. 75. More than 600 million people live on or near an active volcano. 76. Seafloor spreading creates new crust under oceans. 77. Volcanoes form dense, dark glass called obsidian. 78. The Big Island of Hawaii is made of active volcanoes formed over a hot spot. 79. Scientists who study volcanoes are called volcanologists. 80. Violent volcanoes can shoot ash more than 100,000 feet into the sky. 81. Volcanoes take thousands of years to form, but Parícutin, in Mexico, grew almost 165 feet in one night. 82. The rotten egg smell near some volcanoes is caused by a gas called hydrogen sulfide. 83. The eruption of Krakatoa in Indonesia in 1883 could be heard almost 3,000 miles away. 84. One eruption sent pumice flying as far as 16 miles away. 85. The moon is sometimes called "dead" because its volcanoes are extinct. 86. Edinburgh Castle in Scotland is built on an extinct volcano. 87. Wet ash can weigh down a tree enough to make it fall. 88. Magma collects in underground chambers below volcanoes. 89. Earthquakes below volcanoes can sound like thunder. 90. Volcanologists can predict if a volcano will erupt within days or months. 91. Volcanic craters can hold lakes of lava. These rare lakes create a bright red glow at night. 92. Pumice can be light enough to float on water! 93. Most active volcanoes release smelly sulfur dioxide, which has the same odor as a just-lit match. 94. Volcanoes can form geysers—holes where hot water bursts out at regular intervals. 95. Native Americans used sharp volcanic obsidian for arrowheads, cutting tools, and trading. 96. Lava domes that grow too fast can collapse. 97. A submarine volcano can cause a tsunami. 98. Millions of tourists visit volcanoes every year. 99. Venus has more than 1,600 volcanoes. Scientists don't know if any of the volcanoes are active, but they have seen the levels of sulfur dioxide increase in Venus's atmosphere. 100. Volcanoes can cause avalanches of snow, ice, trees, and volcanic matter.

INDEX